The Prince of Horrors

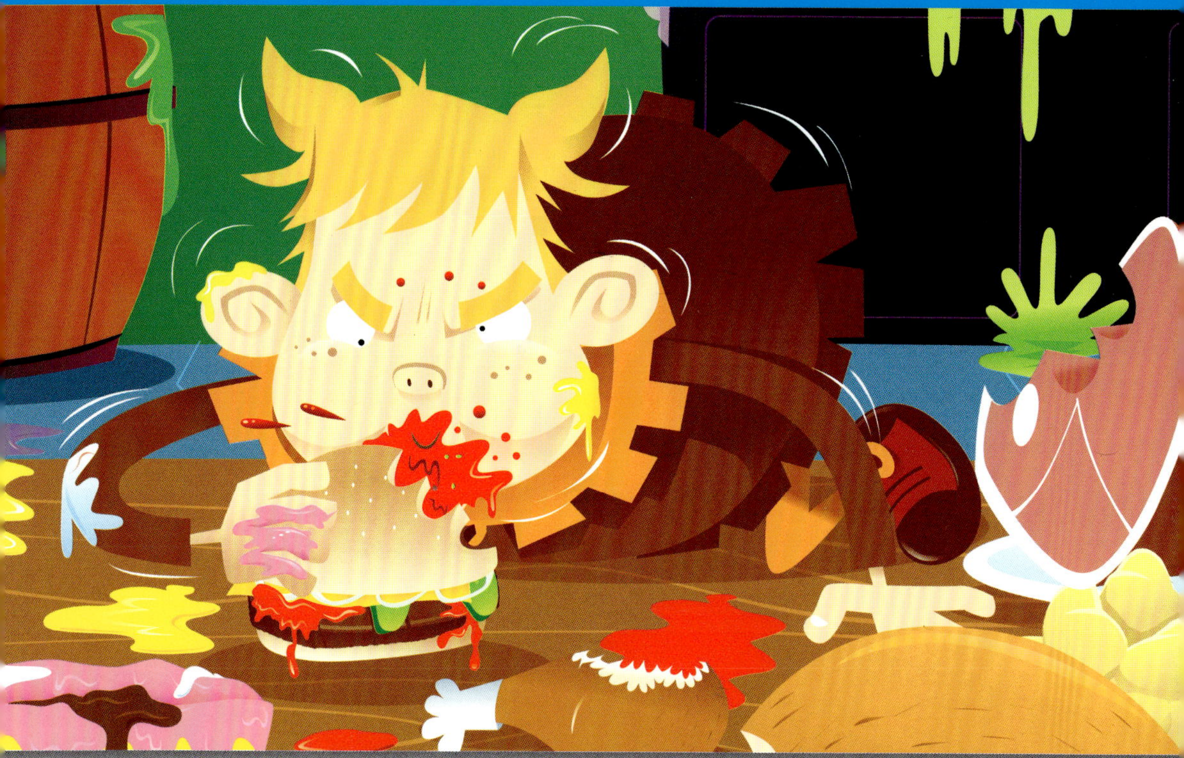

Written by Lisa Thompson
Pictures by Andy and Inga Hamilton

Prince Wilson came to play.

"Be good, my little treasure," said his mother as she waved goodbye.

"I'll do what I like," said Prince Wilson.

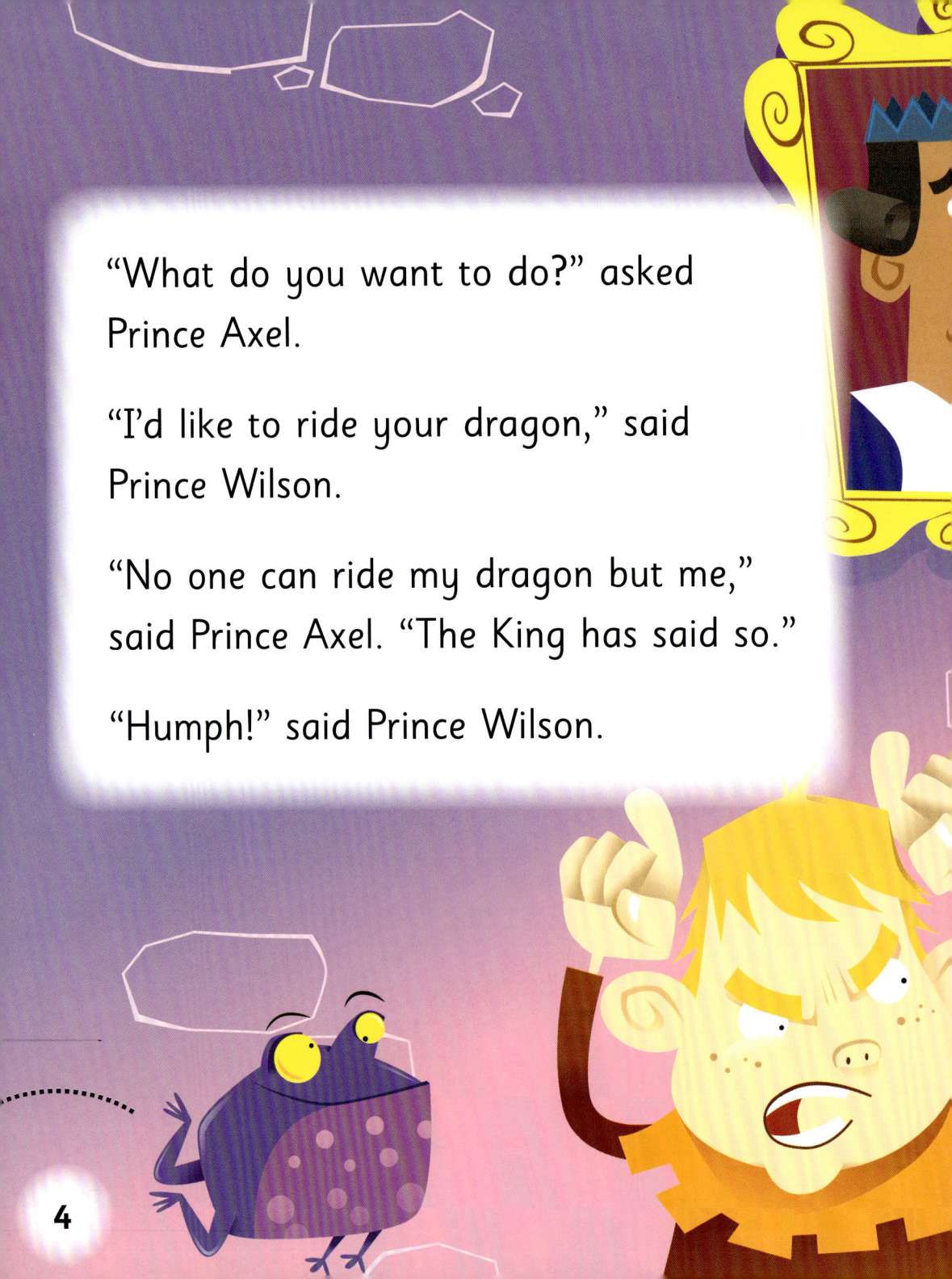

"What do you want to do?" asked Prince Axel.

"I'd like to ride your dragon," said Prince Wilson.

"No one can ride my dragon but me," said Prince Axel. "The King has said so."

"Humph!" said Prince Wilson.

Prince Wilson stamped around the games room.

He looked like a gorilla.

Prince Axel giggled.

"I need to ride your dragon," said Prince Wilson.

"No one can ride my dragon but me," said Prince Axel. "That's the King's order."

"Humph!" said Prince Wilson.

Prince Wilson ate everything in the kitchen.

He looked like a greedy monster.

Prince Axel chuckled.

"I have to ride your dragon," said Prince Wilson with his mouth full of pie.

"No one can ride my dragon but me," said Prince Axel. "That's the King's written order."

"Humph!" said Prince Wilson.

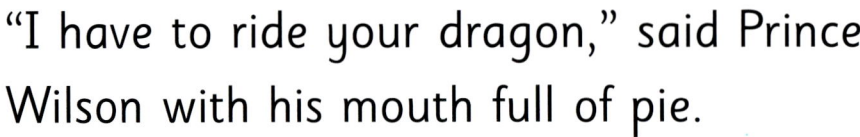

Prince Wilson complained that the swords were too heavy for fighting.

He looked like a squawking chicken.

Prince Axel laughed.

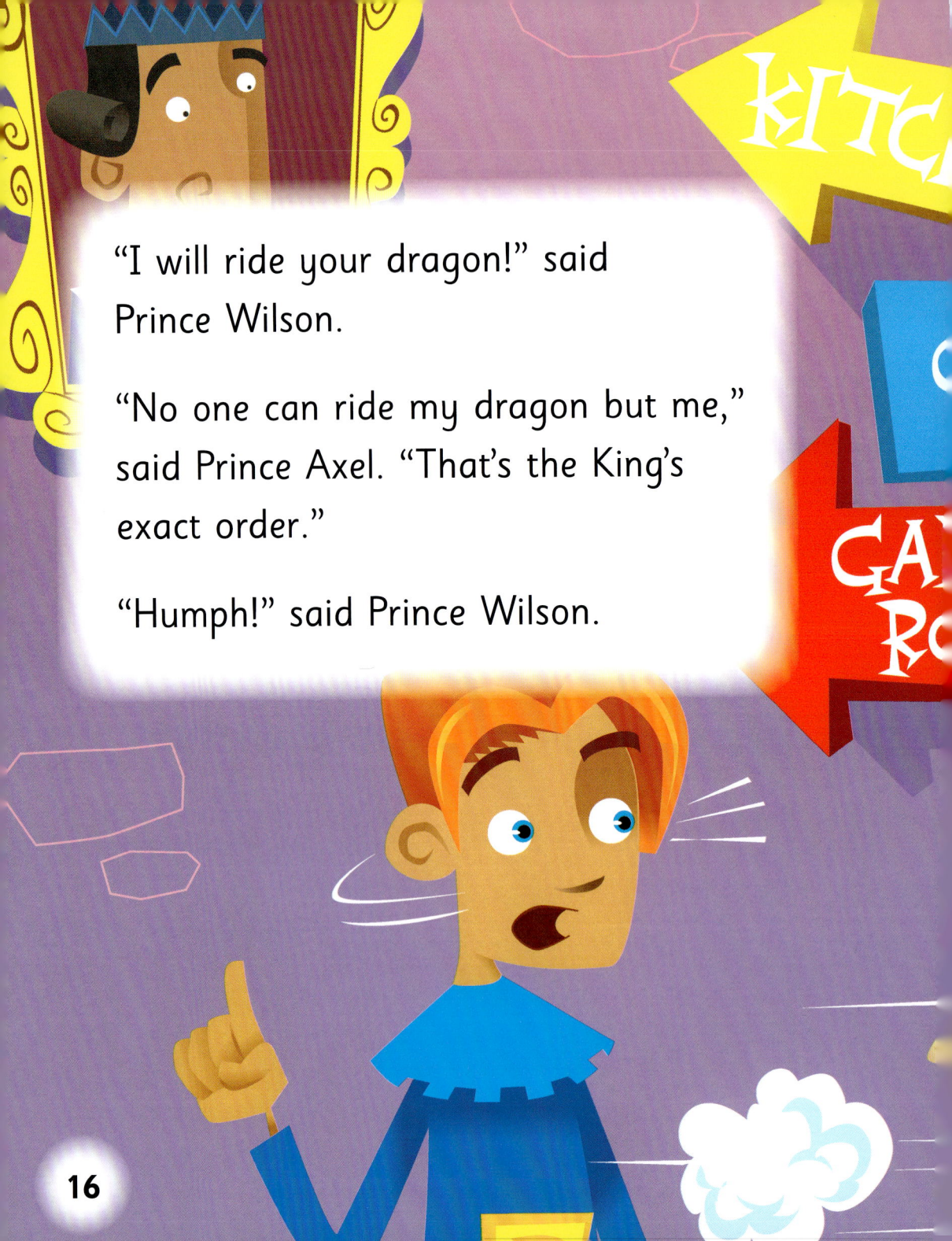

"I will ride your dragon!" said Prince Wilson.

"No one can ride my dragon but me," said Prince Axel. "That's the King's exact order."

"Humph!" said Prince Wilson.

"I'll do what I like," said Prince Wilson as he climbed into the dragon's den.

"Stop!" cried Prince Axel. "No one can ride him but me."

"I'll do what I like," said Prince Wilson.

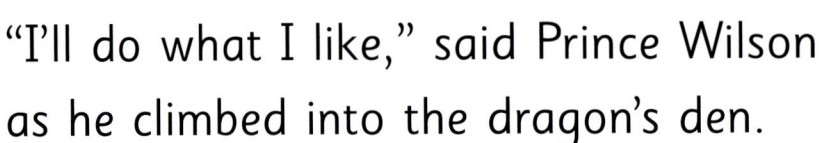

Prince Wilson climbed onto the dragon's back and told him to fly.

The dragon sped off. It did not like being ridden by Prince Wilson.

"Help! Help!" cried Prince Wilson.

Up and down, faster and faster the dragon flew.

"Heeeeeeellllllllpppppppp!" yelled Prince Wilson.

Out came the King. He ordered the dragon to land.

Prince Wilson fell safely to the ground.

"You will not do what you like in this castle," said the King. "That is a direct order from the King!"

Prince Wilson never asked to ride the dragon again.